MW01515674

KIDS IN
TRIAGE

KIDS IN TRIAGE

Kilby Smith-McGregor

A Buckrider Book

Buckrider Books is an imprint of Wolsak and Wynn Publishers.

Cover: Stock images from iStock.com and Freeimages.com
Author photograph: Laura Jane Petelko
Typeset in Capita
Printed by Coach House Printing Company, Toronto, Canada

Canada Council   Conseil des Arts
for the Arts   du Canada

Canadian   Patrimoine
Heritage   canadien

ONTARIO ARTS COUNCIL
CONSEIL DES ARTS DE L'ONTARIO
an Ontario government agency
un organisme du gouvernement de l'Ontario

The publisher gratefully acknowledges the support of the Canada Council for the Arts, the Ontario Arts Council and the Canada Book Fund.

Buckrider Books
280 James Street North
Hamilton, ON
Canada L8R 2L3

Library and Archives Canada Cataloguing in Publication

Smith-McGregor, Kilby, author
Kids in triage / Kilby Smith-McGregor.

Poems.
ISBN 978-1-928088-12-7 (paperback)

I. Title.

PS8637.M63K54 2016   C811'.6   C2016-900677-8

Contents

It is a violence from within
that protects us from a
violence without.

Wallace Stevens

Black Matter

Turned the hose on the universe in her bikini and
summer screamed like a kettle. Black matter, black matter;
honey badger, river horse. Daughter of billboards
gummed by spume-wrecked brothers, landlocked, an upright
bagless. Ghost cannons creak the air, effaced; lost dogs
in wheelchairs telegraph behind. Captain's helm spins, fire-
eater's wanton. Black matter, black matter; call Iphigenia
over: out-scream the cattle. Goats and sheep and dust mites
herded in circles, wet-T-shirt pert and wakeful. Bluish
emissions of life from nostrils all night. The horses restless.
Come back to the backyard with the hanging baskets.
Attend the hippo's yawn, the groaning iceberg's offer. Love,
abhorred by abacus-keepers, predestination's trash.
Summer screamed like we all scream. Ice cream; rope burn.
Rope burn; gasoline.

Readings on the Philosophy of Colour:
Morningside Heights

how can this elaboration
            Colour Concept vs.
                        Colour Experience

the model of multiple inscriptions
            news to Newton, yet
                        blackout remains blackout

Battle of Harlem Heights predates
            Bloomfield Asylum
                        Single Room Occupancy

cum SoHa, Columbia's
            gentrifictacular dog fight
                        (*Variantes de la cure-type*)

before George Carlin's
            "White Harlem" or fêted
                        interpretive medicine

Morningside protests
            narrative temporalization
                        sit in St. Luke's and see

the kids in triage since pre-
            Washington's plaster abolition
                        sometime-split-off, the symptom

we grew up out of
            cuticle-bit survivalist roots
                        veining Manhattan schist

see: "The child as projectile"
        a science of aging bruises
                proves speculative at best

afterwardness – what she
        came up with, laughed
                snapping the binder clasp

on my copied pages
        carved a graphite blue
                pain into my forearm

flicked her No. 2
        toward the fountain
                we all welt puce, eventually

defiant, submissive, from B-29
        bomber bays launched by
                and for our mothers, brothers

discharged blind
        no beforeness
                but God, she said

see: DSM
        BDSM –
                autoplastic processing

Wake Up Remembering Oranges

Wake up remembering oranges and I
curl, count to ten, roll off your sister's cot,
compose a list of things we need to buy.

You're in her kitchen, with that insurance guy
I guess, but I can't face you, this, my nerves are shot.
Wake up remembering oranges and I

slink upstairs, root out the weed I know is there, get high,
rediscover the reasons I stopped smoking pot,
compose a list of things we need to buy

to start again, like toothpaste, a new house, try
to conceive of combusting in flame – not
waking up remembering oranges, and I

try singeing a little hair, daring myself to cry.
What's burned can be bought, learned. I can be taught.
Compose a list of things we need to buy.

Remembering oranges, not gas left on. To lie
a little – easier than I thought. The shock
of waking up.
            Remembering oranges, I
compose a list of things we need to buy.

Practice

Descartes dreamed the approach of a man holding a melon, recorded this
in detail, and we once lived in a brick house with a back plot budding
the black earth sweet until it turned.

Dug from the heart of a walled garden, the offering
of complicated fruit. Thin-skinned, translucent, swollen
or nutted in slick wax halves and spiny, flown across oceans
to be bathed in this city basin, bruised to all tastes by clean hands.

In pre-med you practised, pulled an orange first:
Remove the coloured cap from the syringe and draw
the plunger back. Submerge the tip in ink and aspirate,
then load under pressure between your two fingers, thumb.
Hold up to a light source and flick the barrel to force out any air.
Practised until you could feel the correct amount of pressure to apply
in entering, always remembered that skin is tough and will resist the needle.

I think of you now as I wash fruit, triangulation
of your thumb and fingers inside my resistance.
Every pore an injection site, sore, and the late sun
in my kitchen bitten off, tourniquet between teeth.

Untitled (NO RADIO)
after Barbara Kruger

---

[1] BE THE MAN

Fixed from some great distance, silver halide
glint of all my Hippocratic apparatus.

Life is short and Art, long.

I reach for the bottle. I reach for the knife.

[2] STEALING CARS

Thug kids. Romantic. Our self-scarred New York pre-empting NO RADIO
Sharpied in windshields. Of course we'd never boost anything
that couldn't be spared. When I

stuck my fingers in your slick ears, I could touch
hot wiring. When we shuddered in the backseat –
permission freely given: sure,
smile, but don't blink.

[3] OUT OF BODY

Paste jewel in the hologram, bloodshot. Arm's-length
self of foreshortening photographs. Honey –

This can hardly be the whole of us, can it?

Vantage the late-revived relate, that perch of death
carved from the Greek: *see for yourself.*

[4] CRIME SCENE

Caught at the cookie jar, fist thrust
through this window now fumbling for the latch.
Apprehension of sirens, mother's voice scolding –
sweets not prepared for me.
                    Lunging pit bull in my chest; its choke chain
busts. Each jacketed rib snaps. And every jar and bottle, smashed.
Erect, that fine all-over fur of flesh, fresh crumbs
of glass cleave to it.

[5] EXPOSURE

Snapped into sharp relief,
my immaculate Y
incision
now recast as gash.

[6] CAN IT, SISTER

Poised over chest aperture and
in my hand your heart involuntary
muscle

wails.

[7] COOKIE MONSTER

And I, the baboon-headed, jackal-headed, falcon-headed
man, canopic priest –

no Anubis, rather, Janus-faced. Burnt-out eye of the dog, still
blinking. Begging. Sing to me. Sing me *obscura*.
Sing the farther, darker room.

[8] PIRATE RADIO

Cocked head attending
a marble chamber's mouth.

Brow furrowed, straining
for the frequency.

APOCRYPHA

First, do no harm.

Listen,
I only just wanted so awfully to see.

Amputation, Shotgun

They drove home to no radio, her feet
up on the glove box, bracing, head hung
out the window like a loopy dog in summer.
Carving back roads, spit and ping of oiled
gravel against the undercarriage
its own conversation.

After BBQ, canned Blue, she tabled it and they
sat under that constriction of sky, side by
side, reversed on the picnic bench breathing
out over the back forty like all their lives.
Worn knees of his dark work jeans
lined beside her light ones.

If that doesn't work they cut it off, she said
and he nodded, thought of the long, smooth
stalk of a rifle flinting in a saw's dry teeth.
Behind his eyes the whole horizon caught
fire from it, them trying to run together but
her halved, tipped over in the dirt.

He wakes before dawn, erect at the dark
field's edge, steps into man-tall corn, pulls
silk from an ear bearing packed beads of gold
like teeth, one burnt one rotted in the gum.
Bends down to pluck a stick from the furrow
and snaps it over his thigh.

It's not nothing. It's not nothing after all.

Meantime she wants to wear slutty short skirts
she decides, but owns none, so they go to town,
try on new tube styles and A-lines and bias-cuts.
Each hugs, clings or only skims his girl's shape.
Soon talk, treatment, but she naps in the cab
with her feet on the dash for now.

Dundas as Paris is Philadelphia

Sown in REM the spectre of cardiac surgery, a black Ram's
hood cracked, jawed cables roping yolk across snow.
Terror of being stolen, owned, another; wiring problem:
risk adversity. *Nous nous souvenons* dawn awareness

drawn from bookshelf, sump pump, strata of this lent bed.
An anatomical heart driven north from Reading Terminal
Market declared in full upon returning, dark chocolate.
Easter falls when we observe it – no?

Snowfall demands both axe and shovel. Several panes
of the greenhouse have shattered in weather, so –
Think of deer, how they reach with their heads toward
versions of spring. Surviving the French Revolution

only to be born, year one, on a shard-laced back acre.
Neck hung low, pulse threads distal *in extremis* protanopic
both placental, ectoplasmic – already a red/green blade
whetted where we lie before we wake. Off Market St. below

the Liberty Bell, Episcopalians practise Wendell Berry
practise resurrection goat-furred, plaid-quilted, visited
in purples of an ordinary Sunday *nous nous souviendrons*
another country's corrective humour's ache.

Roused to *Wheat Field with Crows,* tracts of killing snow
cleared – salt-lickers, their hosts – beating bounds here
where hearts drank, outlasted night, accepting; long shot,
late-painted, raised to ourselves visions unknown/beheld.

Postcard from the Volcano
after Wallace Stevens

When least we knew our house as breathing will –
the literate part will say gutted. And guess at,
as autumn foxes left what cries

grapes in quick frost, the mansion's
budded left. Our will of bones made with what left look.
Children in sharp white

shuttered beyond speech became our gate to a still-
dirty, storming world; it will by their still-felt despair
speak the tatter.

Picking up for these, we, out above what is,
know aureoles there – once spirit-smeared – blank.
On clouds we never had spring, never gold.
And what of it?

We children of, we look as if and much is left:
our bones, the hill that saw; the windy were of things;
peaked smell; long, weaving blow; the said air
a being and opulent in He that with these, lived.

Know what house that mansion of sky.
That mansion that behind the sun, a sharper more,
seems of shadows.

This Tract

Cirrus in aspic. And below, the horses
      specks, same as childhood. Different
horses, all those horses long-since dead,
      I'm sure we outlive them somehow.

Standing at dusk on the shingled peak,
      pitched at the edge of sky's pliable
glass – a cutlass – my colours
      compared as to those of a snake.

Once God's voice split the beams
      of this house. I return as a horse.
In the casings of paintballs, cut
      panes of a gingerbread nativity.

In match heads and sandpaper,
      biting planed faces. This tire-ground
gravel – the sound – all our
      codes broken down to roads.

A tract not unfrequented. Sheer of skin,
      a still-coiled rope in the corner.
Few conjure it. Her collagen helix
      shattered in some speaking accident.

Letters from Home

My children come to me in the desert
like letters from home, their mother's
hand tattooed beneath the skin, the smell
of her soap on their liminally sticky limbs.

They age narratively with the arc
of her relationships, plotting
the wide mouth between two countries,
points of departure between myself and him.

My children come to me in the desert
like boreal snow, reprisals slow
to melt, revealing tawny wings
protecting spotted breasts of cactus wrens.

They want bicycles, they want their own rooms,
they want to get away with everything
because they have been punished once for nothing
and carry that bruised entitlement:

a hard wooden boomerang flung out at me
across the sand and arcing back
to smack their own soft skulls. My children.
Two months a year.

From the Artist's Private Collection

[1]   The advice of transportable water: yes. But mirage keeps step with salt and soft and perishable – the mess of you, exception and rule. All moving. As I was not, so I was, too, shocked by winds, cracked whip of another's childhood, defiant tail of an electric fence sped through sung dares and laced fingers. And like another other's childhood fingers: drawn, drawing rather, the pattern that rolls and rolls and rolls the grained face of this heat, threading morning's thrift-store boots in their forward cant. Our criss-cross. Fret of expectation and erasure.

[2]   *...required to frack a single well,* he whispers, F-word polished hard. The pressure. The neck, the knot, the beating wing. In the vision I'll be Baltic. Stalk from the pool lit amber, beaded in gooseflesh, embodied double-blind and all tan. Subject and object of a lens-flare afternoon. No amulet pitted with nautili; no exoskeletal eyelash trapped; some other placeholder – then impact that spiders from splinters to ash. Now nothing without setting. The Arabs, French, English, find a generator abandoned, elicit suspicion, harbour her charge. Begun in your sleep, I was marking cards.

[3]   Only over land is the real remembered. By which I mean measured. By which I mean faceless; by which I mean post-form – I mean CO_2-scarred – by which I mean F-less; by which I mean lost. Durational performance, discovered. Each adder, asp, curve, keyed perfectly. Witness for the macro-chronology. Of the animals to which the bones belonged. Almost universally broken. By which I mean damaged; by which I mean: changed. Rock bed like a rack beneath you, pegs that tune and tune until – the song – or someone claps. Match the vellum to the monument; go ahead, rub.

[4]   White handkerchiefs pegged on the clothesline. Stained
      upholstered seats. A child's harness, a cut sheet, causal.
      Strung up's the expression – hairless meniscus, drum's
      hide paling, unpasteurized occult. O plus A minus B
      minus AB plus B plus O minus B plus A plus AB – pulse.
      First they enlisted the cubists to fool us with surfaces.
      Bags of oranges, phone books: cover. The acid-pink blood of
      America in her, blinding plain sight. In place of every wave
      there was a wake. Subtle bodies, chipped polish, old neon,
      appropriations of the dead. This vehicle shrapnel beneath us,
      sprung heat on the clutch.

[5] Supposing truth to be a woman. Remember her to me,
     redwood climber, red object ball. Sheath, sinew, stealth;
     the hunched night's accordion unfurling like a banner
     from the tallest tower, tribute. Kneeling in pleated skirts,
     condescending wet cheeks to old oak. Midas-Tiresias
     moonwalks with a gilded stick: diamondback flung down
     to slither off, knowing. Enter the double doors of J-school in
     drag, hooded, wolfing marrow through a bar straw, dark's
     artery's radius. Molten on felt, an upside-down volcano's
     leavings. Ulna cued. The red ball. The corner pocket.

[6] Now I know what it's like when the head is cut off the body. Nicked in the neck by a Cartesian dualist; would again touch herself and recognize – the severed held aloft and level. Dazzle by water. Ribbons of flag fed back through mouths enunciating the bends. Cat's cradle robber caught up in the hair elastics of girls, a briar rose. Racist comic; naive rapist; hand-coloured film strip expulsion. Resist. In the nave, the apex, a stutter, occlusion – cannon in the magazine magazine magazine – quote bee-stung unquote about the lips.

Witness: Cambridge, Mass.
for Elliot Kravitz

Oh, material. The bride wore red; the groom wore white
     and Elliot Kravitz lived as he practised – a witness.

Bag of blood. The ram's end. Redress before I'd met him.
     Lady novelist arrests before the proffered, diaphanous.

The old men, the young women, the Greek stature. Elliot
     Kravitz as Hippocrates. Elliot Kravitz's hippocampus.

Watched him teach her how to stand again, ascend, to walk
     the unknown forward.   Metastatic as means:

removal or change – *an entrance which upholds and shores*
     the stone-crush up the air like lace. Mass made idea,

and idea held in place. My surgeon's high arches, I marry
     you. In place of every scar, a handmade bead. Seeded

embers of address across the bodice of the living. Stays of
     repossession. Communion faces chosen in need

and promise. I'll see you at the lectern. Burnished crown, new-
     blistered brow; commitment. A kingdom slaked in it.

On the Occasion of St. Valentine's Death

Finally he was beheaded on February 14, AD 270
An old priest who did not heed the edict:
                    No more marriages

He did not cure the blindness of the jailer's daughter
            Let me disabuse you
                    Did not write her letters signed ——
            He was not her lover
Maybe taught her how to read or maybe nothing

Amateur anthropologists in wishful excavation
Apologists – insinuate secretions
            Lips perforated, lacy, along dotted lines
        Flesh summons signed
        In lonely fingers' animate desire:
                    – Your Valentine

        The shape of the heart is not the shape of the heart
But February is cold enough

In the church of St. Anton: his cervical vertebrae
Downward displayed in a glass-fronted baroque case.
            Suddenly earnest, an American tourist
        Takes off her shirt, wraps up her fist, smashes the glass,
        Plucks out a rib to pleasure herself with

                First he was stoned
            Finally beheaded

If she remembers him as her lover
If she believes he has cured her blindness
        It is not because she has
                A memory of love, a belief in sight
                    A letter signed ——

Piecework
after Patricia Lockwood

For all her life she did piece work
        on the orange assembly line, she tied
awful flesh knots at the ends of oranges
        to separate one from the next,

played Cash's cover of "Hurt" over
        in her head and owned the scut, casing
of her hours among machine parts,
        a rosary. At times a navel

protruded, at times it withdrew into wax.
        At times her fingers over the hatch
of the flush grid muffled more
        than singing. Oh, for want

of a refractory pony and an event
        horizon to ride toward. For want
of a sister, bleached cotton,
        a coffin, a mister, two fingers.

For all her life she'd known how
        to avail herself of a vacuum.
To little–, or, *to no–*
        The orange grove's abandoned

rectory reeks of rinds shed and darkening
        low walls beneath a cantilevered flap;
mucus-streaked sky's recalcitrant
        crust, man imagined in black

and he leaned down and told how the air
       drilled a hole in her to breathe,
and he leaned down and told how the red
       spiraled off in one neat piece.

What weight? she asked, as the belt
       conveyed the paring through a hose.
And she tied it off as she'd been taught, *to no–*
       knowledge-rendered fat implacable.

Like the lie of oranges in a sausage factory,
       of girls and horses, rainbows, prolapse.
Extract in the afterwax. Hairnetless,
       to the wall, steel-toed; belly button

piercings infect only themselves,
       Lord knows. *To little–, to no–*
For the life of her she abandoned
       on the orange assembly line

awful flesh knots, rough sectioned ends
       of oranges, plaited strains of "Hurt"
in her original's cover
       of a unicorn.

Adam's rib its horn. Right blasted.
       Her humming forehead's own
fist soldered, machine
       parts the core.

Red

Red is the lining of my mouth, my cunt, my favourite coat –
      well, pink in the light and red at night.

Sometimes silk.

Red carries blood on its back through the snow.

Red is wet and heavy. It is naked, inside-out.

Set on fire, skinned alive, red is the currency of desire.
      Red demands payment. Violent birth and violent death.

Red lace panties.

A glut of mortality. Red seduces.

It will perform, not necessarily as you wish.

Red is the taste you're seeking that doesn't exist. A jewel
      swallowed by a monk in the Middle Ages –
      he felt pain as it passed his heart.

Now we all go to God with red in our bellies.

On our heads. Our hands. Red is a burn, a brand.

Red is emergency without infrastructure, I have seen it
      on the news. An engine, an assertion. Red is means,
      red moves.

Red pools.

Red glances.

Red glares.

Red is a reflection, a fetish, transgression. Red dresses
a theme of sharp points.

Red eyes: bruised wells, betrayal of the photographer's flash.

I'm sorry but it's anger.

Red crosses. Even in love.

It is history and injury. The history of injury.

Masculine attention.

Medical attention.

I will not go on about wounds, scars protracting the red–white
continuum through time.

This is not a productive conception of time (toward white) –
it is a concession.

Someone else's idea of healing.

Yes, the apple.

It was a Red Delicious. Even the flesh was red,
blood apple. They write that out of the Bible.

White is an invention of History.

Room 257:
I Eat Your Ice Chips

Nurse folds you forward like a lawn chair sprung to sitting,
civil-disobedience slack stunned out by blunt fingers, sticks
of dynamite jammed into cracks, sparklers until.

A crackerjack unwrapping of your paper gown, but the last
Russian doll holds at least a dime-store promise – your twitching
rib cage; nothing, honesty. Concave, hairless-cat nakedness
    that can't be glossed.

Cheap opacity of lacquered wood, hack primaries – desalinized
want, watching a stranger strip you with complete detachment.
Nearly sick in the sharps bin beside the bed, I swallow the thick
    of my knuckle's gnawed mass.

Everyone needs something to cure, you're sure of it. I'll try harder
than I've tried for life to laugh. I will spit ice chips at back-turned
white coats for bull's-eye points, say, *suck on this.*

Summer and shine and sneakers, the spin of things, when a sick
stomach is a sign of good, elastic capacity, commitment to naive and
deep-coursing appetite – dizzying, knee-scraped, feuding, forgiving love.

Once your mother dressed you. Not like this. She dressed me too.
And I can red my frost-cut tongue electric like a fire engine
because I have been a child and know how to hope.

Taking Off Your Glasses

The slip-through trick of cufflinks
like coins through water, you
unbuttoned, creased and folded.
Jackknife cut of elbows jutting,
cocked, sure wrists into hands-up.
Ready man in his shirt sleeves
then. A pang like biting tin
conducted through my fillings,
sunk mercury eyes.

Your hands in my hair, paws,
fumbled. Whisky kiss plugging
my ear to itself, sense-stopped
in my long-dead uncle bent down
to press about how was school.
Since when do you drink that stuff?
I asked, unlooping my entanglements
with your fingers.

Since when do you care? You grin
at me, between nibbles along the arm
of your gunmetal bifocals, slide
yourself between comforter and sheet.
River of lye beneath. Who will come
to soap us, to crush our last bone hulls
by hand? What was it I harboured?
This act of taking off your glasses
still signal for some war.

[1] PAYMENT IN LIQUOR CIRCA MID-SIXTEENTH
THROUGH EARLY NINETEENTH CENTURIES

Dowse the gunpowder with spirits. If the powder will not ignite,
the spirits should be considered under proof and any payment
in this form a cheat. If the powder does ignite, pray to God, pull
back your fingers, remember this is what you asked for, strength.

If there is no gunpowder on hand, substitute something combustible.

DE INCENDIIS CORPORIS HUMANI SPONTANEIS, 1763

You think me a terrible person but you did not know my wife.

She was a drunk. Cold. Last observed unable to sleep, shuddering
through the upper corridors barefoot, muttering she must, she must
go down to the kitchen to warm herself.

Let the record show the remains of Mme Millet in an unburnt chair.
A portion of skull, particular vertebrae, her lower extremities.
Let the record show *visitation of God*. That will silence anyone.

It was finally the young surgeon, Le Cat, who said it. Who convinced
them of how this could happen. Because of this man,
I have been acquitted.

Let the record show what I have been left with. Her lower extremities.
Particular vertebrae. A portion of skull. I did not go down to the kitchen.
I never heard her cry out in the night.

You presume a science of fire, but you did not know my wife.

Acetone, formaldehyde, she melts me retinal. Oh, Penny Dreadful!
What's it then you feel to drink?

This feral full-bodied's the new bicarburet – suspicious as gingers,
as sexy, as witches, as syllables' plattered savagery, the smut of
bootblack in back of your throat. Don't pretend a mind weren't
pre-set, meted out hospital-corner precise. Who taught you so?
There'll be no more dancing girl. That's the punishment for pettiness,
Penny, for my serialized thoughts: *The Tears of Jacob Faithful.*

Polymerized, ephemeral, skittering along the arc –
ashes, ashes,
    blown iris in the egg.
            Cast of liquid past in ideation.

I carry a torch.

[4] WHY ARE YOU STILL LOOKING AT ME (NOW)

Whiteout. Every him I touched her. Every time I touched him
oh-so-feminine bottle. Every time I was touched, lips. Every time
I looked, was she looked at
                    through
                  or over.

I want ammunition. I want proof of life. Hack off those appendages
and keep right on sending them. Of course I want payback, my plans,
my carriage, my taste. I want my taste. I want my memory. My taste.
The young surgeon. My bloody halo, but that only happens after and
it's never really over. I can make you a crime with my mind. A fistful
mouthful. A thousand lightnings every hour of care it takes to fit her.

Let's make the trade. Strike me your future.

More Heat Than Light

In the future, incandescence is over. Inefficiency
is over.   The future is bright.
                Some spots in Scandinavia,
the future has already happened
and they are sending dispatches back from their state
of compact fluorescence.   We never knew
        what it was to be so cool and blue,
        they say, so much history has been wasted
over heat, spinning
                    on spits above fires without an ounce
        of foresight, so many lifetimes
butted up against one another,
        baking,
        hot and sad.
                    Thank God, I think, *we will not
        have to burn forever.*
What a hard lesson learned for Western Civilization.

*

[Before now, when my grandmother fell asleep smoking in bed, so many times, it was just dumb luck those sucked red cherries did not pop like clots in the folds of her close blankets, that the oxygen of her anger was smothered before a wick effect could take effect in her wadded fat, the inside-out of her candle self. I think. I think I can safely say that my grandmother did not spontaneously combust, even as she dashed full plates of food against her husband's broad-shouldered stoicism; it was only the slop of sauce and guts, never electrical issue.

They smoked separately, outside their bodies, trying to ignite themselves ON in the dark. "My smoke could speak to your smoke" they might have hoped; however, the cigarette does not comprehend the pipe. But it is at an interminably slow speed that the wick effect, in fact, proceeds. Swaddled fetal pigs and fatty pounds of flesh, as control groups, prove only the possibility of murky yellow flame and much production of soot over more lapsed hours than anyone could sustain the concentration to count. Hardly enough glow to read by, even.

It could have simply been a sunset, the kind of haze that coats a city belching itself. There was no fire to put out. It could be wrong of me to remember my father's mother as an un-slippered foot at the base of the striped recliner. Twin charcoal knobs of fibula and tibia pointing up like pens uncapped. A foot and maybe a shrunken skull dropped softly onto the grey dandruff of entirely eaten breasts and spine now dusting the taut seat cushion. It is wrong of me to place her husband there on the occasional table: cast Lucite vase that slouched toward her during the event, re-forming bent but memoryless while the rest of the room remained intact ——

—— to make a cruel affair between incineration and contortion. To trade Kitchener-Waterloo for Pompeii with the presumption of the living over the dead, sifting through scatter for teeth, seeking.]

It is only a kind of story I try to write myself toward the light switch.

*

In the future, it is not like this. In the future
we have achieved distance.

Edison's Dream

Edison's dream of me is imprecise. An hourglass upended, blood rushing to the head, flooding measure of a half-life more heat than light. He wants to smooth my points to curves between his broad, wet palms, spin me on a wheel with his knife at my hip to carve out the coil, the gesture, potential, the rest fallen in a ribbon of fruit rind. Current in this body, both organic and unnatural, cut or thrown, switch of a knowledge still waiting for thought. Edison's dream of me is Michelangelo wresting a woman from a block of ice, bit tinfoil filament. It burns him. In the morning his hands are thick with scars. There is no math for it, no exact science. Of the two of us it is I who have the advantage. I am the one who remembers the dream.

In the Study, I Cannot Say How

I am watching this man who has been a teacher for many years
clean his Italian pen with the name of a woman.

Body twisted gently open, expertly unthreaded, a soft rag drinking
left ink as it blooms unanswerably black between his fingers.

Autumn bends over the desk and he is bloody with it, hanged afternoon
cross-hatching loose leaves, their cursive mouths struck through with light.

Only now overcome by the weight in his hands. Sunset.
Foreknowledge of winter. Only mouths. Open vowels
in unhoused darkness.

Embolism and sob, unseated, rising then seized between desk and doorway,
flooded rag clutched in a flattening dusk. Folded to the thin carpet,
grasping. I meet him there. For the first time

I am watching this man who has been my lover for many years
rip at the buttons of my blouse for a memory of his mother.

Provenance
(not another *Mona Lisa*)

Rising stiff-necked from between
folds of centuries, you have lost
weight, freeze, oil-pressed
in the seat of your war with this
landscape of icebergs –

I miss the glow of open
breast most of all, a sternum
worried away under
strokes of editorial cartoon,
heavy-hooded colour Xerox –

You know to withhold is the right
choice, as pink-tipped rubber
hugs your cheek, seeking bones,
sliding through like a hot knife,
you know –

On Sawing a Woman in Half

In every town, in every turn toward,
known –

by jig saw bowsaw buzz saw
                    split, restored.

Gapped cutwork, whitework,

        bloodless wonder,

            spit of bone and string, half-
hitched, bit-knotted.

            Neck wrenched toward
grins, caked lids drawn wide, letting

to the keen crowd of knife-eyed
oglers, stragglers clenching tent poles.

            Inch toward and elbow into.

            Her eye, a slug of red:
please –
let the trick finally end, let
        the cut finally bleed.

            Tatted heirloom lace
of skeined hair training to the stage;

            all splayed and bare
box of her, framed.

...it's not English anymore, it's not getting squeezed through any hole.
— **David Foster Wallace, "Good Old Neon"**

[1]   Cry me a little match girl, matchless before
the boy who crushed through keyholes came
confessing. His heart, pure as the driven.

And he could bend a spent figure to grief:
words so blunted, jawed back, upchucked
all but dead, delivered – the breaking grace
of a scar-ugly thing stripped to its base
intelligence.

Love, she'd struck, who'd never hoped
to read like that, and be written.

Oppenheim's Object

It is not so difficult to extend the arm with ink,
to name the wheel incisor, lollipop guild or iron lung.
The age of barber-surgeons once again looms: red licorice
and rust-clotted napkins, offset. Death to the screw press.

It is not so difficult to extend the hair, or any part,
indeed, with names. If the blade slips. If we like the taste.
The significance of her rubber bracelet?
It's all for something – or against? I meant to ask.

In the basement of the college, yes, there is a printing press.
Take your snuff shots. It is not so difficult to extend
the latex down the shaft. This machine is eons old
and it still stops at every floor, but let's make

our business birds, not cages. 24-karat-crested swears
which wheel the wind and wing the damp tunnels,
visioning extractions. The cyclist wanted a sporting chance.
It is not so difficult to be an Alice, epoxy – or forgotten outright.

It is not so difficult to make the fur adhere. There is
no such thing. Trussed bootlick, finger-pointer – Oh!
Who doesn't adore the small world song? Those electrified
figures waving flags of many colours. Come, huff with the Hatter,
ride the teacup a little longer.

One died just now in childbirth, so –
you-know-where, I guess. Your equator's showing.

Opened a detailed colour pamphlet.

Participated in this freaky west-side theatre intervention.

One said a definition of *everyone* made me viscerally, laterally bent, or –
vomit-headed if we're being – if we're being – *being*, here.

One died between the heading and the subhead,
black-hooded.

One lived to ninety never counted, yet untouched.

You know how one was burned up one elided one was slit up one was
stoned down river one elided one survived to face the corner,
wear the helmet, stroke the link-by-link of fence.

One bent to catch my mother's mother's vomit.

One bled out holding up my social platform's tits.

Embarrassment of riches.

No one sharked at the post office. No one skipping class to work.

[3]   You open your mouth, she turns
Battery and citrus blossom

Elaeis guineensis, ether cleavage
Leave autumn and the reconstruction
Go

[4]   Adamantine, automatic, semi-
High-proof lubricant

Broken down, dead-dropped in sand

What pardon claims this
Beautiful excuse for a history professor
His vestigial

Morphogenesis
for Alan Turing

By birth your hands: the church, the steeple; code
of ordination, edifice, oracle, orifice, ordinal sequence
of *mouth curves lie curves light cuts marble.* Then our lad-god
hung from the headboard embroidered by tongue, by touch, a man-
to-be, sped: sluice of stars down a garden drainpipe – escaping – logic
of night scythed and sieved for last kisses. Awake. First fist-broken

ordinance, this new contingency. Now each exponent *sweat broken*
back breaking skin broken sin of hosts and old boys' code
for nailed-to-the-wall – penetrable – this double-agented logic
of bare forearm semaphore, invisible eloquence; closed sequence
knotted in cuffs, at throats. Initiate operative, witness a flagged man
meet his violence, in illness extinguished, stilled teenaged god.

Yet every Cambridge, every set of oxfords raises a fresh god:
everything that is the case against you, the world broken
down to *words between wars between words between man*
and his mirror, the master. Anti-realist vet vs. Government Code
& Cypher School; Guy's vs. Bletchley; dick measuring sequence:
those high gilt zeroes and ones run through to the hilt with logic's

sharp. These days it's seamlessness; embedded logic
of razor-blade apples, pills, chips slipped beneath skin to out-god
even the notional *autonomic gnomic gnostic mimic* – sequenced:
an evolutionary narrative's lithe tail, forked and broken
over a war's chair's back, chained to pipes, to pixel-ratio, time-code
plus today's paper evidenced in the frame-by-frame of *X* man

thought known (or lost). But for his work, we would have lost. Man
cum man again. One of the fathers, if not the father. Coffee cup, as logic
demanded, yet chipped and handle-chained to retrospect regenerating code.
Mouth broken wars mimic words between sin (and his master?) God,
that talented long-distance runner. Enigma, Oracle, Machine. Broken
syllabics bent over the face of the fairest of speculum sequences –

a kind of cold rhyme. Fruit flesh wound. Specific sequence
of shutdown valves and pulmonary constrictions stripping man
to a fairy tale of his own sleeping, his bit knowledge, his beauty broken
cries sky-strikes and skin stipples on last nights in solitary logic.
No snow but sand. No face but face. No go but go. God's
feature in profile. Dust's profile in code.

Chapter II: The Pool of Tears

I wish I hadn't cried so much... I shall be punished for it now,
I suppose, by being drowned in my own tears.
  – **Lewis Carroll, *Alice's Adventures in Wonderland***

[1]   The river of my childhood is the Speed River. Starting near
      Orton, Ontario, it flows south through the city of Guelph.
      Archivists have described it as wide, shallow, rapid,
      unnavigable – also: a source of power. That seems about right.
      The river that runs just beyond the view of my window.
      The one where I have caught crayfish and cast sticks to watch
      them be whisked away. Living on Rural Route Five
      in the lower half of a large split-level which had once
      been a school, I sit at my small desk by this window
      drawing a series of trap doors in a green Hilroy notebook.
      It is an illustration for the kind of Alice story that consumes
      a certain span of youth encompassing coming into the world,
      and is later returned to, looking for a way out.
      I wish I hadn't cried so much.

[2]   The screen door sighs and clicks shut behind me.
I follow my feet down the hill along the edge
of the property to the lower fence cut from spruce.
I mount it like a horse and kick over, flakes of russet
bark, like scales, still clinging to the insides of my thighs
with the dying sensation of all my weight taken between
my legs. I bear the impact of the drop in my ankles,
their forming bones like upturned screws, securing
the shafts of my calves in place, as if without this little
jolt, its small pain, my feet might have run off
one day to follow their own mind. That coming
down to earth, the monstrous growing, shrinking,
breaking and knitting that followed,
I shall be punished for it now, I suppose.

[3]   There are two routes across the highway before me,
      one above ground, easily imagined, and the other
      underneath. The storm drain, echoing from its mouth
      of corrugated metal, persuades. Because I'm trying
      to get to a place which means hands and knees
      in the dark, the resistance of stones against palms
      and pant legs, closed cold lit by a rip of light
      a long way off. I crawl because the story demands
      my submission, and because underneath the ground
      is a good place to inch forward alone. Because
      I'm trying to reach the river, where I will stand
      tall in clammy boots and feel the current whip and twist
      the eighth-inch of rubber enlisted to protect me from it,
      being drowned in my own tears.

The Blue
after William H. Gass

Let us move our minds as we must,
a common deer in her winter coat;
the taking of the whoreship *Cyprian*.
From the blue, the blue. For form

was once the schoolyard of a life,
your time in her winter, common
worship. The simple boundary
of being, a-swoon or awake,

sighted, in her blue winter coat
crosshaired and reeling. Flush
as salmon, a flock of petticoats.
Creel at your hip, a holster. Her

scramble up the mizzen ratlines
casts you pirate, alas. Those darker
lines like you cast always over
your own *dear dear* breath.

This burr hole, flecked with grease,
suckles a touch at the drill. Let us
pull back our minds – beneath
the dura: ice-black, blood –

slow-draining bath,
            an oyster in a glass,
                    a hook,
                    a glove...

You Meet My Mother Over My Dead Body

Suspension-bridged across the city,
toes hooked on the tired railing
of a balcony at the Isabella Hotel,
fists flown out toward the water
somewhere south, as you cross over.

A woman mouth-deep in Lake Ontario
tries to unlock my hands, dumb knobs
since I stroked out last summer. I cannot
open doors anymore. She looks just like
my mother, but you would laugh at that.

When you get there, when my spine
has fallen away under your spike heels,
star-punctures this night, you must
speak to mother for me, my tongue's still
tied to rocks. Jaw won't open anyway.

Tell her I've tried, my joints are tired –
how you've touched me. Tell her stop
drowning all hours, and I remember as a child
kneeling at the hopscotch of pregnant acts
exacted in chalk, rising against gravity to jump.

Noir Wager
(on the Late Victorian Stage)

Your Borsalino's smudged nap against my stone-skipping
small-blind fingers. My knuckle brass; your gutter-dent

pinch-front snap-up your tearsheet your teardrop-shaped
crown. Rubbed and wished spit whispered upon, trod to

rotting boards. Mark it. These notched reeds were once
diviners, bent to a murmur slow-cut by water or rather

worn that way. Quit silver sinks concentric; body binding
blacker lake. A beer hand. Sarah Bernhardt's Belgian rabbit

or Sarah Bernhardt in tails. Remember Princess Fedora
remember phrenology lumped in a throat's circumference

of head. She tasted sharper decades on, choice delivery –
speech suckered, rum ran. Hold this vase hold this handle

hold this habit raise this veil; *beat my teeth out kick me in
the stomach for mumbling* – called. Verbatim's widow now.

The Wife of the Man I'm Seeing

Gets hold of me in the shower, slides
her fingers down my ribs and cups
my belly from behind. I'm afraid she'll
jam her pinky in my navel and deflate me,
or pry out the umbilical root and pull.

This evisceration never comes, only
the swelling that anticipates a bruise.

Plato's Bruise

And the Republic for which it stands. White beach of
sociopathy crammed with, stripped
of strangers.

Which we christened pristine. His breath too much
flesh stank of unlet blood: repeated.
Reminded us of us.

Watched her toddle off and waved. It is not like in the philosophy
and it is. I envied your tears the possibility
of drink. So struck.

Of course you have. Carved a cross in a circle, dividing;
withdrawn without turning, denied.
Translated:

missing the mark. A killing face. Of course you have landed
wide, welting. Not weighted: physical
laws corruptible.

Marked, ungovernable, yet navigable as if. We were
liquid still, not reflection estranged
by particulate, wave.

Anomalies of Water

Unusually high melting point – boiling point – critical point. Six to eight cups per day. Threshold. Specific heat capacity, unusually high. Eight to ten cups per day. Respiratory system must be moist.

Hot and cold. Water runs. Water shrinks on melting. Now puddle. Now stepped in. Now on the bottoms of boots. Suctioned to the hulls of ships passing in the night. Ninety percent submerged and counting. Unusually high surface tension.

At low temperatures, self-diffusion increases as density and pressure increase. Spread thin, unmaking, disclaiming, un-naming. Water breaks. Warm vibrates longer than cold. Churning. Density increases on heating. Denser than expected, lighter than expected, lightest known.

Breakwaters create safe harbours. Prevent spills. Pressure reduces melting point. Resists thaw. Resists advances. Retreats. Whited-out in storm. Redacted still. Revised inviolate. Carving into wrists and ankles, ropes of water. Cuts diamond with diamond, snow-blind. Exacting. Water revenges.

Number of nearest neighbours increases on melting. Number of nearest neighbours increases with temperature. Water spills against water, crashes into water. Courses. Water sought-after. Water learned. Spitting on the other hemisphere. Molecules move farther away from each other with increasing pressure.

High-spirited, hard-living. High heat of sublimation. Water forgets water. Water refuses water. Water wants wine, transubstantiation. Highlight, high life, high-flying entropy of, heat of vaporization. The eventual condensation of, repatriation of rain.

Muscle: seventy-five percent water. Fat: twenty percent water. Present water. A particular interest in intracellular water. X-ray diffraction shows an unusually detailed structure. The hint of a face. No aqueous solution is ideal.

Amniotic

[1] SWIMMING LESSONS

it's called *egg beater* imagine
an egg beater in the kitchen
an egg beater hand mixer in the back
of the cupboard there's a wheel that
you turn a crank you spin the blades
spin they alternate never touch the blades
of the egg beater they fold in fold everything
together imagine an egg beater unbending
back like fixed to a chair begin
from your knees
kick

keep your palms flat keep
your fingers closed you must
invent a surface your body made flat
must create resistance in the water do you know
what infinity looks like? this is how you move your hands
back and forth both hands like you are spreading
jam on toast in the kitchen spreading
jam on toast burnt toast but underwater
unseen labour that is virtue crack
the egg onto the
cooktop

don't lose focus don't forget about
your legs don't forget about between
your legs they never touch you spin work
your resistance resistance is what lifts you
up work hard we see your chest out rising from
the water it is your strength that keeps
your chest high rising from
the water keep
going

                                        you can do
                                    anything you can
                                be whatever you want to
                            be you must we know you can
                                be this will save your
                                        keep your
                                        head up
                                            head
                                            dn

no, wait, it's not swimming it's something else

[2] TRICKS WITH EGGS

I know an experiment where you can get an egg inside a bottle by setting it
    on fire no that's not it

I know an experiment where you can get an egg to swim in water
    add salt

and there's another egg trick with swimming another experiment I know

an experiment where the egg's unbreakable if you only press
    the right place

I can turn an egg into a mirror not telling trick with
    a candle I know

the difference between hard-boiled and raw one spins better

you can make an egg see-through with vinegar or you can tie a bone into
    a knot try it

also there is a joke about me that all my childhood pets committed
    suicide maybe they were sick this is nothing to do with swimming
    except the turtle the fish and there is another joke about me but I don't
    know it

[3] VARIABLES TO BE CONSIDERED

physical fitness

desire to live (willpower)

familiarity in the water

water temperature

air temperature

current

wind speed

waves

weather

sharks

the cutline is *in space, no one can hear you scream* but I can't remember the movie *just when you thought it was safe to go back in the water* is *Jaws II* they have underwater cameras cameras watching from below

when I was born I broke my mother's body broke in and out when I was born my father missed the eleven o'clock news when I was born they said *it's a girl* so many lessons badges levels testing testing life-saving artificial respiration CPR I never learned to testing testing when God said to Noah *how long can you tread water?* everybody laughed except Noah or maybe Noah laughed too for a while and then he stopped treading water is movement fighting movement treading water is the force of work against work never reaching out efficiency of fear as economy of movement all the fight of keeping your head up cutting itself with all those rows of teeth

imagine an egg beater straight-backed resistance the same motion as spreading jam on toast or patting a dog's head, *good girl*

Of Water

All my blue is not
transferable.   Not an account
                                    of water
not evaporated. All my blue
                    is practice
with a prism in me.

Acknowledgements

Financial assistance from the Toronto Arts Council and the Ontario
Arts Council's Works in Progress program is gratefully acknowledged.
Additional thanks to Mansfield Press and Wolsak & Wynn for their early
support through the OAC Writers' Reserve program.

Versions of some of the poems included in this collection have appeared
or are forthcoming in *Brick, Forget, The Puritan, Matrix* online and
The Malahat Review. My gratitude to the editors of these journals.

Thank you to Sharon Smith and Hillary Rexe for their contributions to
the development of the manuscript, and to Kate Cayley and Jessica Moore
for intelligent readings and friendship.

The creative writing programs of the University of Guelph and York
University have been unstinting in their support of both my writing and
my person – many thanks to their faculty, students and administrators.
I am especially indebted to Rishma Dunlop for extraordinary mentorship
through my early years of wrestling with poetry, and for her singular
flare and vision.

Paul Vermeersch is responsible for the existence of this book on many
levels. I thank him for his generosity, persistence and editorial acuity.
Emily Dockrill Jones contributed a smart, sensitive copy edit. I'm deeply
appreciative of the work Noelle Allen, Ashley Hisson and the whole
W&W team undertake in support of their authors every day. Thanks,
also, to Natalie Olsen for a beautiful book.

Credit, always, to my family and my very dear friends.

Notes

Readings on the Philosophy of Colour: Morningside Heights
references Jacques Lacan's *"Variantes de la cure-type"* ("Variations on
the Standard Treatment"); "The child as projectile," a paper by R.E. Tibbs,
D.E. Haines and A.D. Parent; and the *Diagnostic and Statistical Manual of
Mental Disorders* (DSM). BDSM is an overlapping abbreviation of Bondage
and Discipline (B/D), Dominance and submission (D/S), Sadism and
Masochism (S/M).

Practice contains adapted language from a variety of medical manuals
and online resources.

Untitled (**NO RADIO**) is named for Barbara Kruger's 1998 art piece.
At the height of the crime wave in New York City during the late 1980s,
a peculiar phenomenon occurred: handwritten signs displayed in the
windows of parked cars with messages like "No Radio" to ward off
would-be burglars. Kruger upended the iconic phrase by printing the
statement in bold red text across an ink drawing of a Victorian autopsy
depicting a white-bearded physician poised over a female cadaver
with her heart in his hand. "Life is short and Art, long" (*"Ars longa, vita
brevis"*) is a common translation of the beginning of Hippocrates's
Aphorismi; the aphorism "First, do no harm" (*"Primum non nocere"*) is
apocryphally attributed to, and associated with, the Hippocratic oath –
an approximation can be found in Hippocrates' *Epidemics*.

Dundas as Paris is Philadelphia references the phrase "practice
resurrection" from Wendell Berry's "Manifesto: The Mad Farmer
Liberation Front" and Vincent Van Gogh's painting *Wheat Field with
Crows*, 1890. For Michael and Alex.

Postcard from the Volcano is composed of text from "A Postcard from
the Volcano" by Wallace Stevens.

From the Artist's Private Collection borrows the lines "Supposing truth to be a woman" (*"Vorausgesetzt, daß die Wahrheit ein Weib ist"*) from Friedrich Nietzsche's *Beyond Good and Evil* and "Now I know what [it is] like when the head is cut off the body" (*"Jetzt weiß ich wie dieser Augenblick ist in dem der Kopf vom Leib getrennt wird"*) from Peter Weiss's 1964 play *Marat/Sade* (*The Persecution and Assassination of Jean-Paul Marat as Performed by the Inmates of the Asylum of Charenton Under the Direction of the Marquis de Sade*).

Witness: Cambridge, Mass. includes italicized lines from John Ciardi's poem "Most Like an Arch This Marriage." Dedicated to a remarkable stranger.

Piecework takes its opening and seventh (italicized) stanzas from Patricia Lockwood's poem "Killed with an Apple Corer, She Asks What Does That Make Me?" which sparked its composition. It references the 1994 song "Hurt" (written by Trent Reznor of Nine Inch Nails), which was covered by Johnny Cash on his 2002 album *America IV: The Man Comes Around*.

Spontaneous Human Combustion and Alcoholic Proof samples many electronic records on the subjects at hand. *De Incendiis Corporis Humani Spontaneis* is a book by French author Jonas Dupont containing some of the first case studies of SHC, including the death of Nicole Millet. *Jacob Faithful* is a Victorian novel by Frederick Marryat also featuring an instance of the phenomenon.

Matchbook takes up Hans Christian Andersen's "The Little Match Girl" and serves as an elegy of sorts for David Foster Wallace; my caveat nicked from Russell Green via Malcolm Lowery: "Sentimentality is a name given to the emotions of others."

On Sawing a Woman in Half was inspired by Steven Price's poetry collection *Anatomy of Keys*, which takes Harry Houdini as its subject.

Oppenheim's Object is named for surrealist Meret Oppenheim's 1936 art piece *Object (Le Déjeuner en fourrure)* – a teacup covered in fur, which is housed in New York's Museum of Modern Art.

Morphogenesis is dedicated to pioneering computer scientist and WWII code-breaker Alan Turing, prosecuted for sodomy and subjected to chemical castration by the British government. A suspected suicide at age 41, his posthumous pardon was granted in 2013, nearly sixty years later.

The Blue borrows phrases and feeling from part two of William H. Gass's *On Being Blue: A Philosophical Inquiry*, which in turn references a scene from John Barth's *The Sot-Weed Factor.*

Noire Wager (On the Late Victorian Stage) includes italicized lines from the 1946 film *The Big Sleep.* It also references the premiere of Victorien Sardou's 1882 stage play *Fédora*, which starred Sarah Bernhardt in the title role; the style of hat she wore became synonymous with the name of her character.

Anomalies of Water is composed of text adapted from Martin Chaplin's lecture notes for "Sixty-Three Anomalies of Water" (South Bank University, London).

Amniotic incorporates an unattributed tagline from the film *Alien* and references Bill Cosby's "Noah" joke from his 1963 debut comedy album *Bill Cosby is a Very Funny Fellow...Right!*

Kilby Smith-McGregor spent her early professional life making theatre. Writing across genres, she has contributed to *Conjunctions*, *The Kenyon Review*, *Brick*, *Descant*, *The Malahat Review*, *The Puritan* and *Best Canadian Essays*. Kilby won the Writers' Trust of Canada's 2010 RBC Bronwen Wallace Award and holds an MFA from the University of Guelph. She works as a freelance graphic designer in Toronto.